THE FRICK ART & HISTORICAL CENTER

THE FRICK ART & HISTORICAL CENTER

The Art and Life of a Pittsburgh Family

Mary Brignano

Photography by Duane Rieder
and Frank Walsh

The Frick Art & Historical Center, Inc.

1993

An Interlachen Group Book/Dennis Ciccone

Published by The Frick Art & Historical Center
7227 Reynolds Street
Pittsburgh, PA 15208

Project Manager: Dennis Ciccone
Author: Mary Brignano
Photography: Duane Rieder and Frank Walsh, Rieder and Walsh Photography
Production: Ripinsky & Company
Design: Joyce Weston
Typesetting: Pagesetters, Incorporated
Printing and binding: Amilcare Pizzi, s.p.a.

ISBN: 1-881403-01-7

Photography on pages 10, 12, and 16 courtesy of The Carnegie Library of Pittsburgh, Pennsylvania Division.

Cover illustration: *Still Life* by William Michael Harnett (1848–1892). Oil on panel, 7½ × 9½ in. Purchased from an unknown source by Henry Clay Frick, November 12, 1895.

First printing 1993

Manufactured in Italy

FOREWORD

VISITORS to the Frick Art & Historical Center have an opportunity to enjoy an unusual place on a number of levels. Even though it is first and foremost the home of an important American industrialist, Clayton, the Henry Clay Frick estate, also possesses general significance as an artifact of American social history and a document of American and regional architecture. The estate constitutes a small urban park. Nearby, The Frick Art Museum presents, alongside a permanent, private art collection, a continuous series of exhibitions based upon the latest scholarship. The greenhouse, carriage museum, and grounds exemplify important aspects of life in the late nineteenth century, while a shop displays merchandise related to all parts of the center, and a tearoom offers sustenance and repose.

Everything the visitor experiences at the Frick Art & Historical Center is implied by the character of the place itself. At Clayton, homey values and high culture coexisted peacefully. Both were dear to Mr. Frick. Every inch the *paterfamilias*, he encouraged a family life based upon close relationships and simple values on the one hand, and appreciation of art, literature, and music on the other. Consequently, The Frick Art Museum should be seen not as separate from but as a natural extension of Clayton. If Clayton is a house that contains art worthy of a museum, The Frick Art Museum is a gallery with the flavor of a home.

My first visit to Clayton occurred in late 1983, a year before Helen Clay Frick's death, when the house was still her residence. From that late autumn afternoon, I recall a dimly lit, densely furnished, well-upholstered spit-and-polish interior and the smell of buttered raisin toast in the air.

Paintings—some by great names, more by artists I had never heard of—hung everywhere, not so much for decorative effect as in evidence of avid art collecting. The house was strikingly individual, and, because the rooms appeared so complete in their old-fashioned way, obviously a rare survival from days long gone.

Throughout the restoration, which from beginning to end took four years, all parties responsible—trustees, architects, contractors, and staff—endeavored mightily to preserve the personal, individual character of Clayton. That they succeeded is due in no small measure to the survival of ninety-three percent of the original furnishings and an extensive archive, which documents many aspects of the estate, and, to be sure, Miss Frick maintained the house exceptionally well during the sixty-five years that she owned it. The main tasks were to put everything into proper condition to welcome visitors and to return certain elements of the structure, which had changed over time, to their original appearance.

Meanwhile, in 1985, The Frick Art Museum had begun to present temporary exhibitions. At the time of my first visit to the museum, when I wandered alone through the galleries, the only display was the permanent collection, which seemed suspended in unearthly quiet. Today, while it is still a place of quiet and contemplation, the museum brings to Pittsburgh special exhibitions of art from the nineteenth century and before. Often, these are exhibitions of Old Masters or nineteenth-century drawings, which by their very nature reveal the artistic inception of finished works like many in the permanent collection galleries and at Clayton.

The nonprofit Frick Art & Historical Center carries out the charge of Helen Clay Frick, its benefactress: To foster appreciation of art history and of an important chapter in American social history. We welcome our visitors and hope they enjoy their time here.

DeCourcy E. McIntosh
1993

AZURE SKIES AND GREEN LAWNS

JUST twenty minutes from Daniel Burnham's Frick Building in downtown Pittsburgh is the setting for an experience you will not soon forget. On six parklike acres, green lawns, gardens, and towering trees frame the art and life-style of a golden past. A châteaulike Victorian mansion, meticulously restored to all its nineteenth-century opulence by the region's finest craftsmen, welcomes you. Nearby, a domed greenhouse filled with the mossy fragrance of flowering tropical plants . . . and a transportation museum where you can imagine riding in horse-drawn carriages or a shiny, 1914 Rolls Royce add pleasure to your visit.

Then, in an intimate Renaissance-style art museum—where fresh flowers greet you year-round—you discover a select, personal collection of rare paintings, tapestries, sculptures, and decorative arts—as well as changing exhibitions of art masterpieces, a lively music recital series in a comfortable 161-seat auditorium, and lectures by internationally known authors. In this unique setting you come face-to-face with the pleasures of the arts, history, and landscape. Your pace slows . . . you gaze up at the trees . . . you while away a golden afternoon. You return again and again, if you can, and find something new to charm your senses and stimulate your mind.

A Daughter's Vision

Your entire experience—Clayton, its gardens, greenhouse, carriage museum, and The Frick Art Museum—was orchestrated over years of planning by Helen Clay Frick (1888–1984), the third child of industrialist and art collector Henry Clay Frick (1849–1919) and his wife, Adelaide Howard Childs Frick (1859–1931). An alchemy of art and nature, as well as of Miss Frick's memories of her idyllic childhood, the Frick enclave draws you into her vision of an ideal way of life. It was a life she wanted new generations to understand and to appreciate.

Helen Clay Frick was born and spent her early years in Pittsburgh, at a time when this city was becoming the most important industrial center in the world. As the daughter of a wealthy, influential family who prized art and nature, she grew up with Tiffany silver, Old Master paintings, servants, hothouse flowers, high-stepping pairs of shiny horses, and also with loving parents, aunts, uncles, and cherished friends. Art and nature gave her great pleasure all her life. At the age of only ten, she wrote about her bedroom at Clayton, "There are pretty flowers and birds painted on the ceiling and walls. . . . If all the children had such a pretty room as mine, there would

Helen Clay Frick (1888–1984), seen here at age five and at age twenty-two, wanted The Frick Art & Historical Center to preserve her family memories and her vision of an ideal way of life.

Henry Clay Frick's New York residence at One East 70th Street, built between 1911 and 1914, was designed to display his world-renowned art collection. Planned from the beginning to receive the public, it opened as The Frick Collection in 1935.

not be any of them sad or unhappy." She envisioned her home as a place of "azure skies and green lawns."

Although the Frick family left Pittsburgh for New York in 1905, her childhood home retained a powerful hold on Helen Frick. She insisted, for example, on returning to Clayton for her debutante party in 1908. And while her primary residence remained in New York, she maintained the house in virtually unchanged condition, inviting her nieces and nephews and later their children to visit her in Pittsburgh . . . and through Clayton to learn about their heritage.

The Frick Art & Historical Center is Helen Clay Frick's personal legacy. In donating an art museum and in opening her family home to the public, she followed in the footsteps of her father, whose world-renowned art is displayed in one of New York's greatest private houses, The Frick Collection on Fifth Avenue.

The story of Miss Frick's remarkable legacy begins more than a century ago, at Clayton . . . and with the young couple who moved there in 1882 to raise a family.

THE FRICKS OF CLAYTON

HENRY CLAY FRICK was thirty-two and his wife, Adelaide, twenty-two when in August of 1882 they bought an eleven-room house in the suburbs of Pittsburgh—the industrial colossus then producing two-thirds of the nation's crucible steel. To the Fricks their "Italianate-style" house seemed quite suitable, and the young couple found its location ideal. Here in Point Breeze the air was fresh and clear—with hardly a whiff of the sulfurous smell that once saturated much of Pittsburgh. The house fronted Penn Avenue, about to become "Millionaire's Row," yet the 1.43-acre site adjoined virgin forest and rolling hills. What is now Homewood Avenue was then just a country lane, bright with summer wildflowers. Horses clip-clopped along Penn Avenue, pulling streetcars and carriages, and two blocks away was a Pennsylvania Railroad station. Mr. Frick could breakfast at eight o'clock or earlier, catch one of the frequent trains, and be at his downtown desk in about half an hour.

Mr. Frick worked in this office on Fifth Avenue in downtown Pittsburgh, the city he helped to make into the steel-producing capital of the world.

Married just eight months, the Fricks had been living in an apartment in the Monongahela House, downtown Pittsburgh's finest hotel. But now they were expecting their first child in March, and they wanted to establish a real home. They wanted a private, comfortable refuge, far from the tense, gritty world of business, where they could nurture their children. It would be a haven they could decorate with beautiful, carefully chosen things, and where they could live out the sort of family life idealized for all the world by Queen Victoria, Prince Albert, and their nine children.

In 1882 the Fricks paid $25,000 for the house. They bought it from the widow of a plant manager for Carnegie Brothers Steel Company, Mr. Frick's new business affiliation. They would spend another $50,000 on architectural renovations and furniture.

Thirty-one-year-old Henry Clay Frick first saw Adelaide Childs at a Pittsburgh party in 1881. He insisted on an introduction, and they were married six months later.

The Fricks paid $25,000 for their house in 1882, when Mrs. Frick was expecting the couple's first child. It looked this way until its major remodeling in 1892.

They could certainly afford to hire a good architect and to order from New York the most fashionable furniture, wallcoverings, draperies, and rugs. After all, he was the "Coke King," the *wunderkind* from Connellsville who had resolved to be a millionaire by the time he was thirty. A brilliant, methodical organizer. An adamant, iron-willed "thinking machine" whose blue eyes could quickly turn icy. An affectionate and thoughtful husband. A reserved, handsome, well-dressed man who, wrote William L. Mellon, "could have served as a model in manners." An art collector who had insisted from his teenage years on owning "the best there is."

Henry Clay Frick was born December 19, 1849, in West Overton, Pennsylvania, a farming village forty miles southeast of Pittsburgh. His father, John W. Frick, was an easy-going farmer. But his mother, Elizabeth, was the daughter of Abraham Overholt, a shrewd Mennonite whiskey-distiller, landowner, and miller whom his neighbors called "the squire of Westmoreland County." Clay, as his family and friends knew him, grew up under the influence of the stern patriarch of the industrious Overholt clan.

At the age of twenty-one, he recognized that opportunity lay in plentiful Connellsville coal . . . the soft, sulfurous, bituminous coal that could be slowly baked into "coal cakes"—coke—and shipped by rail to fuel the modern Bessemer furnaces of Pittsburgh's growing steel industry. Boldly, Frick borrowed money and formed a partnership with two cousins and a friend. In 1871 the firm of Overholt, Frick and Company started business

in Broadford, along the Youghiogheny River near Connellsville. To finance the construction of fifty beehive coke ovens, Frick took the train to Pittsburgh and applied for a loan of $10,000 at the new bank of T. Mellon & Sons. Its founder, Judge Thomas Mellon, sent an agent to investigate the young entrepreneur, and his report reveals the practical, down-to-earth judgment of a nineteenth-century Pittsburgher. "Lands good, ovens well built, manager on job all day, keeps books evenings," observed the agent tersely. "May be a little too enthusiastic about pictures but not enough to hurt; knows his business down to the ground; advise making the loan."

Despite the financial panic of 1873, Clay Frick sold more and more coke in Pittsburgh, and used the profits to buy more and more coal fields at depression prices. He bought out his partners. He bought out his chief competitor. He lived frugally. Gambling on the return of better times, he built hundreds of new coke ovens. And by the late 1870s, when the tide of depression finally ebbed, when coke rose in price from ninety cents to a dollar a ton . . . two dollars . . . three . . . then five dollars a ton . . . the firm of H. C. Frick and Company dominated the coke market. It had nearly a thousand employees and as many ovens. It shipped a hundred carloads of coke a day to Pittsburgh.

At the age of thirty, Henry Clay Frick had made his first million dollars.

By the time Mr. Frick was thirty, he had achieved his goal of becoming a millionaire. His coke company shipped a hundred railroad carloads of this important industrial fuel to Pittsburgh every day.

Adelaide Howard Childs married Henry Clay Frick on December 15, 1881—one day before her twenty-second birthday.

Now he changed his frugal, rural life quite dramatically, perhaps living out dreams long deferred. He traveled to Europe. He moved from Broadford to downtown Pittsburgh in March of 1881, spending $5,000 in three months to furnish a $200-a-month apartment. At Tiffany & Co., for example, he paid $850 for the onyx and gilt bronze clock and candelabra displayed today on the parlor mantle at Clayton. He also bought *Landscape with River* from the nationally recognized western Pennsylvania artist George Hetzel. It now hangs in Clayton's reception room.

It was at a Pittsburgh party in 1881 that Clay first laid eyes on the young, pretty Adelaide Howard Childs, daughter of a shoe manufacturer. "I want you to introduce me," he immediately insisted to his friend Andrew Mellon. But in the formal etiquette of the times, Mellon felt it would be more proper to find an older person to bring the two together. Propriety triumphed: six months later, on December 15, 1881, the Childs-Frick wedding became "one of the most notable of the season." The bride wore ruffled ivory satin; a lace-trimmed veil; and diamond earrings, a gift from the groom.

Landscape with River, by George Hetzel, is Mr. Frick's first recorded purchase of a work of art. He bought the painting on February 12, 1881, for his first apartment in Pittsburgh.

In New York for their wedding trip, the couple was invited to a luncheon hosted by Frick's biggest customer, Andrew Carnegie. Carnegie, eager to secure for his Bessemer furnaces a steady supply of coke at the right price, used the occasion to propose a new partnership. The infusion of Carnegie capital made Frick the largest coke manufacturer in the world . . . and began the often stormy partnership between the ebullient "star-spangled Scotsman" and the close-mouthed Clay Frick. By 1892 Frick would organize the sprawling Carnegie interests—mills, mines, and transportation facilities—into the largest steel firm in the world. Frick's business relationship with Andrew Carnegie would last for two decades. It would bring him great wealth and opportunity . . . and also frustration, anger, anguish, and a narrow escape from death.

Andrew Carnegie and H. C. Frick entered into a business partnership in 1882. Their stormy, immensely profitable association would continue for two decades.

Adelaide and Clay Frick moved into their new house early in 1883. She gave birth to a son, Childs Frick, at home on March 12. Two years later Martha Howard Frick was born, and on September 3, 1888, Helen Clay Frick.

By 1890 the Fricks realized that Clayton was no longer suitable for their three children, live-in servants, and assorted dogs, ponies, birds, and rabbits. Mr. Frick was now chairman of Carnegie Steel, and his relatively modest home no longer reflected his increased importance in the steel capital of America.

And so in 1891 they called in an architect, twenty-six-year-old Frederick J. Osterling. Born in Dravosburg, Pennsylvania, he had a passion for extravagant, ornamented buildings from the romantic European past. He first proposed remaking Clayton into an enormous approximation of a French Renaissance château. Although the Fricks insisted on scaling down this grand scheme, they did like the style, popularized in New York by the American architect Richard Morris Hunt. In 1891 Osterling began to transform the eleven-room, two-story house into a twenty-three-room, four-story mansion.

By 1888 the Fricks had three children: Childs, Helen Clay (in her mother's arms), and Martha. After a long illness, Martha would die in 1891.

The Fricks moved out for the remodeling—but when they returned the next year, they were in mourning. In July 1891 their beloved little daughter Martha, whom Clay Frick called his "Rosebud," had died after a long illness. She had been in constant pain for two years—an agony for any parent, helpless to relieve a child's suffering. Martha was buried in Homewood Cemetery. From Clayton's new fourth floor, in winter, when the leaves were off the trees, the parents could make out her small grave.

A Tragic Homecoming

When the Fricks came home to their "new" Clayton in late January 1892, Mrs. Frick was again expecting a baby. Mr. Frick was preoccupied with business: He was about to culminate his reorganization of the Carnegie interests into the world's largest steel firm, the Carnegie Steel Company—a limited partnership capitalized at $25 million and employing more than 30,000 workers. And at the Carnegie's Homestead Steel Works, the labor contract with the Amalgamated Association of Iron and Steel Workers would expire on June 30. Before Andrew Carnegie left the United States for his summer holiday in Scotland, he instructed his chairman, H. C. Frick, to pursue a hard company line against the union.

The events of that summer would profoundly affect labor relations in the steel industry for years to come. . . and the Frick household as well. At Clayton, nineteen-year-old Anna Marie Blumenschein, whom the Fricks had hired to help in the household, lived with the family during these unforgettable months.

Anna would recall fifty years later returning home with the Fricks in the winter of 1892: "Remodeling had been going on for over a year and was still far from finished. The interior decorating of walls and ceilings was still in progress. Parquet floors had to be sanded and polished; woodwork had to be finished; shades, curtains, and draperies had to be hung; imported china and bric-a-brac were carefully handled and put in their proper places. All was confusion throughout the house."

In 1892 H. C. Frick's brilliant organizational skills forged the Carnegie Steel Company—the largest steel firm the world had ever seen. Carnegie's modern works along the Monongahela River became the site of the notorious Homestead Strike that same year.

PITTSBURG, SUNDAY MORNING, JULY 24, 1892.

THE SHOOTING OF H. C FRICK.

A Natural Result of the State of Lawlessness Which Has Recently Prevailed at Homestead.

On July 23, 1892, as the Homestead Strike continued, Alexander Berkman burst into Frick's Pittsburgh office and attempted to assassinate him. Newspapers around the world carried the story.

Meanwhile, tensions continued to rise in Homestead, the mill the Carnegie Steel Company was eager to make the most technologically advanced in its empire. This mechanization, however, would eliminate jobs and force change upon the work practices of the Amalgamated, one of the country's strongest labor unions. While the Homestead Strike cannot be explained in one or two sentences, the chronology of events tells us that negotiations between the company and the union broke down in late June. Determined to continue producing steel, the management hired Pinkerton guards to maintain access to the mill for nonunion workers. When the Pinkertons arrived at Homestead by barge at four in the morning of July 6, shots rang out and a twelve-hour battle ensued. Ten strikers and three Pinkertons lost their lives.

Two days later, on Friday, July 8, Mrs. Frick gave birth to her fourth child, who was named Henry Clay Frick, Jr.

Homestead became headline news throughout the world and H. C. Frick a vilified man in many quarters. A twenty-one-year-old Russian-born anarchist named Alexander Berkman traveled to Pittsburgh, intending to assassinate the chairman of Carnegie Steel. Bursting into Frick's downtown office on Saturday afternoon, July 23, Berkman shot and stabbed him before being subdued. Frick never lost consciousness. He dictated a cablegram to Carnegie, signed several letters, and completed other paperwork. He also gave emphatic orders that no alarming reports were to reach Mrs. Frick, who was still in bed following the birth of her son. Only then would he consent to be taken home in an ambulance.

Eleven days later the Fricks' twenty-six-day-old baby, Henry Clay Frick, Jr., suddenly died. "For the first time since he was shot," wrote one newspaper, "Mr. Frick did not read his morning mail. He laid it aside wearily, saying he had no interest in it. Mrs. Frick," continued the story, "is in a prostrated condition."

THE tragedies of 1891 and 1892 would never be far from the thoughts of the Frick family. The family would dwell at Clayton for thirteen more years . . . affectionate years punctuated by frequent visits of family, friends, and famous people; the day-to-day management of the large house; and the raising of their two children, Childs and Helen. Mr. Frick would stay on as chairman of Carnegie Steel until 1900, and in 1901 he would play a crucial role in the formation of the world's first giant corporation, United States Steel. In the twentieth century he became an active investor in railroads and other businesses. He pursued art collecting, bringing beautiful objects and paintings first to Clayton and later to his houses in Prides Crossing, Massachusetts, and New York City. He died in New York on December 2, 1919.

After 1901, when Mr. Frick played a crucial role in the formation of United States Steel Corporation, the Fricks spent their final years in Massachusetts and New York. They spent time with the children of their son, Childs, and Mr. Frick collected great art. Here he is seen riding in Central Park with the art dealer Roland Knoedler.

"THE DEAR OLD HOME"

YOU CAN see at Clayton—perhaps more closely and accurately than at any late-Victorian house anywhere—how one prosperous family lived during the 1880s and 1890s, when Pittsburgh industries labored to make America's economy the largest in the world. Clayton's $5.8 million restoration, paid for entirely by The Helen Clay Frick Foundation, began in 1986, two years after Miss Frick died. It took four years and some two hundred skilled artisans from twenty-two firms in the United States and Europe. They did their work under the supervision of Thierry W. Despont of New York, associate architect for the restoration of the Statue of Liberty. "Clayton has extraordinary richness and craftsmanship representative of the best of the Victorian era," Mr. Despont has said. "I wanted to put back as much as possible—the smells, the sounds, the flowers . . . the spirit of the house."

"Clayton," wrote Susan Mary Alsop in *Architectural Digest*, is a "triumph of restoration." Rarely have restorers had access to such complete documentation as they discovered at this house. Miss Frick, who had long intended her "dear old home" to become a museum, changed little at Clayton during her lifetime—and the meticulous family and staff had saved virtually every receipt for the purchases of paintings, furniture, carpet, draperies, and wallcoverings from 1882 on. Seventy-five interior photographs were taken around 1900.

When you step into Clayton, you leave today behind . . . and experience, for a little while, "the kind of life that was lived within its walls."

Step into the Past

Clayton reveals how a prosperous Pittsburgh family actually lived during the late nineteenth century. The restoration of the house began in 1986 and took four years and some two hundred skilled artisans from twenty-two firms in the United States and Europe.

One hundred years ago, visitors entered Clayton through the carriage entrance as you do today. Passing through a surprisingly narrow stair-hall, they received their first sense of the interior in the entrance hall, with its walls, furniture, and portieres designed *en suite* by the architect, Frederick J. Osterling. Perhaps they noted the Fricks' interest in new architectural materials such as the frieze made of Lincrusta-Walton, a specially embossed paper that resembles tooled leather.

If visitors were arriving for an evening party, they might also catch sight of a little red-haired girl peering through the bannisters upstairs. The Fricks' daughter, Helen, loved to watch her parents' guests . . . "the ladies in their lovely gowns and wraps, the gentlemen in their high hats and top coats."

In accordance with formal Victorian etiquette, the Fricks greeted their visitors in the reception room. Careful research—such as examination of threads attached to nails—reveals that this room was redecorated four times in its history. The custom-designed rug goes back to 1892. The gold damask on the walls reproduces the fabric installed there in 1904. As in other rooms throughout the house, the variety of details; patterns; rich, complex colors; and *objets* on every surface are characteristic of the Victorian and Edwardian styles. Visitors could see they were in the home of people who valued current style, quality, and artistic effect—but also comfort, practicality, and restraint. No gold-plated pianos would be found here, as at other homes of Pittsburgh millionaires.

The reception room also served as a gallery for Mr. Frick's growing art collection. The paintings you see here reveal his evolving taste, beginning with *Landscape with River* by George Hetzel (1826–1899), a German immigrant to western Pennsylvania. This meditative scene is one of many landscapes Hetzel painted at Scalp Level, a mountain retreat in Cambria County. Mr. Frick bought it for $260 in 1881—the thirty-one-year-old collector's first recorded art purchase. Within weeks he also bought the anecdotal salon painting *Une Révélation*, by Luis Jiménez y Aranda, from the

In Clayton's reception room, the Fricks received guests formally and displayed paintings from their art collection, which expanded as Mr. Frick began to collect more seriously in 1895. Works in this room include the humorous *Une Révélation* (listed as *In the Louvre* in the family's records), purchased by Mr. Frick in 1881. On the right is *Still Life with Fruit* by Jan van Os (1744–1808), the collector's first "Old Master."

Mr. Frick bought *La Fermière*, his first pastel drawing by Jean-François Millet, in 1897.

New York dealer William Schaus, as well as other European watercolors in a very traditional, often narrative style.

Mr. Frick purchased the first of his "Old Masters," the luscious *Still Life with Fruit* by the eighteenth-century Dutch artist Jan van Os, in 1896. His collecting intensified throughout the 1890s, when he bought many works of the Barbizon School, French artists known for pastoral scenes painted out of doors. *La Fermière*, the first of nine drawings the industrialist acquired by Jean-François Millet (1814–1875), illustrates this phase. He bought the pastel in 1897.

The Barbizon works mark the foundation of what would become one of the greatest and most discerning private art collections in the world, culminating in the Rembrandts, Bellinis, and Titians of The Frick Collection in New York City. And while art collecting was widely popular among the wealthy in the late nineteenth century, as a means of displaying the buyer's familiarity with "culture," Mr. Frick's collection was notable even at the turn of the century. Helen Clay Frick remembered that "when foreigners came to Pittsburgh, Clayton was one of the homes they wished to see. My father was too busy to afford the luxury of returning home to meet these guests, and as neither he nor my mother spoke French, I was called upon to do the honors."

The Dining Room

From the reception room, Mr. and Mrs. Frick would lead their dinner guests across the hallway into the dining room—where you can fully appreciate Clayton's 1892 redesign. Everything in this room—woodwork, mahogany furniture, stained glass transoms, rug, silver-plated lighting fixtures, embossed leather frieze, and velvet draperies with their leather strapwork and aluminum bosses—was designed by the architect. The mood is romantic and Celtic . . . like something out of a historical novel by Sir Walter Scott, one of Mr. Frick's favorite authors. The Fricks selected this style from designs Osterling presented in watercolor renderings.

Heightening the effect is *Consolatrix Afflictorum* by Pascal-Adolphe-Jean Dagnan-Bouveret (1852–1929). When Mr. Frick bought this unusual painting from the French artist in 1899, no wall in Clayton was large enough to accommodate it, and so the Fricks placed it against Osterling's

The Fricks' architect, Frederick J. Osterling, designed every decorative element in Clayton's dining room—preserved remarkably over more than one hundred years. The dining room provided the setting for family dinners, Sunday suppers of chicken and waffles with friends, and historic entertainments—including an eight-course luncheon for President Theodore Roosevelt in 1902.

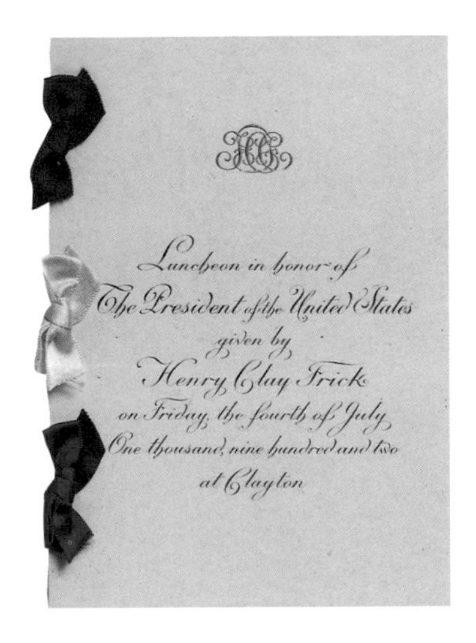
Luncheon in honor of
The President of the United States
given by
Henry Clay Frick
on Friday, the fourth of July
One thousand, nine hundred and two
at Clayton

brick fireplace. In 1990 local craftsmen spent 2,800 hours re-creating the original carved mahogany frame, which had been lost.

President Theodore Roosevelt sat at the dining room table on July 4, 1902. The occasion was a luncheon for men only—as women did not yet have the right to vote. Among Mr. Frick's twenty-one guests were Secretary of State Philander C. Knox (a Pittsburgh attorney), Andrew W. Mellon (later Secretary of the Treasury), and the industrialists Henry W. Oliver and H. K. Porter. The meal was a typically Edwardian cavalcade of *eight* courses, beginning with melon and proceeding through consommé, radishes, salmon mayonnaise, sweetbreads with peas, filet of beef, new potatoes and asparagus, roast duck, tomato aspic, cheese and crackers, vanilla ice cream, cake, coffee, fruit—and appropriate wines. Newspapers also reported on the flowers, "a massive centerpiece of orchids from Mr. Frick's conservatories and 285 of the rarest American Beauty roses" shipped from Washington, D.C., and Chicago.

The Fricks also dined together as a family in this room. Mr. Frick usually came home from work at six o'clock, and Helen Clay Frick would recall that "we dined at 6:30, partly on my account. My father and I sat at one end of the table, my mother at the other. During the meal, the orchestrion played his favorite tunes, among which were the following: selections from *Tannhaüser, Martha, William Tell, Largo*, Gounod's 'Ave Maria.' " The orchestrion, a sort of automatic orchestra, is the same you see and hear today on the enclosed porch. At dinner parties, Mr. Frick enjoyed surprising guests by saying to his butler, "Ask the orchestra leader to play something." In a moment they would be amazed to hear violins, French horns, tympani—all emerging from the music rolls of the orchestrion.

Miss Frick also wrote of her father's favorite foods: Stewed chicken with waffles—a favorite Sunday dinner—home grown asparagus, ears of corn, rare steak served with plenty of salt and pepper. "He liked clams too and fresh mackerel, and with his steak he usually took fried potatoes. *Papa* didn't indulge much in sweets, but fresh peaches and grapes (Concord especially) he loved. He always took a generous helping of spinach, which he called 'the broom of the stomach.' "

The Fricks' meals were prepared by a chef, Spencer Ford, and served each evening by a butler and a dining room maid.

❦❦❦

The Parlor

Formal dinners ended with a temporary separation of the sexes. The women "retired" to the parlor for coffee while the men remained in the dining room to smoke cigars and drink a glass of brandy or port, after which they "joined the ladies." The Fricks used their parlor for many different social events, such as small informal card parties and music recitals. The furniture, all on casters, is easily moved around.

The Tiffany clock and candelabra on the mantel are the ones Mr. Frick purchased for his bachelor apartment in 1881. The velvet wallcovering, a reproduction of the original fabric, was woven in Italy and embossed in France. Surviving untouched, however, is the burgundy velvet frieze, dotted with mother-of-pearl sequins applied with silver thread. The reupholstered sofa and chairs are among the first pieces the Fricks bought in 1883.

The survival of this furniture and fabric may be due partly to Mrs. Frick's meticulous housekeeping—in the 1890s a task similar to directing the activities of a small business. Chambermaids not only cleaned the furniture and art objects regularly but also changed the parlor and other

Guests gathered in the parlor for music recitals, card games, and visiting. The Fricks bought the sofa and chairs in 1883, and Mr. Frick chose the clock and candelabra set on the mantel for his first Pittsburgh apartment in 1881.

The music on the piano, "Il Primo Bacio" (The First Kiss), is dedicated to "Mme. Frick."

rooms with the seasons. Removing the draperies and portieres each summer, they slipcovered the upholstered furniture in white, took up the carpets, and laid rush matting on the parquet floors. As a child, Helen Clay Frick looked forward to the return of Clayton's winter apparel. "Early in November," she remembered, "the house was transformed by having the winter draperies put up and it took on such a cozy, warm appearance."

The Kitchen

Clayton's servants made the kitchen and butler's pantry the scene of bustling activity throughout the day. The staff included a butler-valet, Mrs. Frick's personal lady's maid, the children's governess, the coachman and stablehands, the chef, two chambermaids, a dining room maid, a laundress, and gardeners. In 1896 their combined salaries totaled $419.25 a month. The butler, head gardener, and coachman each earned $60 a month, the chef $40, and the live-in maids between $25 and $17.75. Here, "backstage," they prepared food, received tradesmen, polished silver, washed dishes and glassware—and kept an eye on the annunciator, the electric signaling device the family used to summon a servant.

The Breakfast Room

The family ate informal meals in the breakfast room, using the custom-made, monogrammed Eastlake-style furniture purchased in 1883. They ordered the furniture when Mrs. Frick was expecting her first child, and the baby's high chair shows that the Fricks intended their children to be very much a part of their lives. This was unusual, because most upper-class parents did not bring their children to the table.

The room's unusual wall treatment—plaster work framing aluminum leaf—shows the Fricks keeping up with the latest Pittsburgh technology. An affordable method for making aluminum was discovered in this city in 1888—and Mr. Frick's friends the Mellons invested in its manufacture. They helped create the company known today as Alcoa, the Aluminum Company of America.

Peaches, the painting by American-born, European-trained G. W. Waters, was chosen especially for this room and has probably hung as you see it here since 1892.

The breakfast room is also where the industrialist held his weekly after-dinner poker games. His daughter recalled fondly that "I had the important duty of arranging the chips and took great pleasure in doing this, feeling my part was a very essential one. Those who came regularly were Philander C. Knox, David T. Watson, Andrew W. Mellon and his brother, Richard B. Mellon. . . . The following morning, the room still retained the odor of the cigars which they all smoked."

Hall and Stairwell

At Clayton, even the stained glass "art" windows told a story. These romantic literary heroines are Miranda, from Shakespeare's *The Tempest*; Isabella, from a poem by John Keats; Marguerite of Goethe's *Faust*; and Madelaine, probably from Keats's "The Eve of St. Agnes." The windows date from 1903–1904.

Walls decorated with aluminum leaf, a monogrammed high chair, a nineteenth-century Chinese porcelain vase, and *Peaches* by G. W. Waters are among the individual delights of the breakfast room, where the family ate informally and Mr. Frick played poker with his friends.

Mr. Frick's bedroom, with its maple woodwork, original wall stenciling, mahogany furniture, and family memorabilia, is surprisingly understated. In his private room, this "captain of industry" and art collector placed pictures of his wife and children.

The unusual chandelier originally burned oil and candles. It was converted when the Fricks electrified their house in 1888, perhaps at the urging of their neighbor George Westinghouse, who founded the Westinghouse Electric Company in 1886.

Bedroom of Henry Clay Frick

Anyone who knew only the tough, iron-willed business side of Henry Clay Frick would have been amazed at the bedroom you visit today, with its array of family pictures. Because upstairs at Clayton, away from the peering eyes of guests, Clay and Adelaide Frick lived a close, affectionate family life in which the love of children clearly took center stage.

By Victorian standards, Mr. Frick's room is simply decorated. The bird's-eye maple woodwork is beautifully carved, but not elaborate. The art in the room consists of a few early purchases. In his most private room, this knowledgeable art patron looked at pictures of his wife and children. The largest of the children's portraits is of his daughter Martha, his "Rosebud," who died in 1891 at the age of six.

This is also the room where he recuperated after an assassin tried to kill him during the Homestead Steel Strike in July 1892.

The most luxurious niche of this private space is Mr. Frick's bath. Added in 1897, the room has its original silver-plated fixtures and nickel-plated plumbing, the latest technology of its day. The curved door matches the window frames of the bedroom . . . while the domed, stained glass ceiling admits light from above.

Connecting Mr. Frick's bedroom to his wife's is a small area he may have used as a dressing room. One of the two telephones in the house was first installed here in 1883, when a telephone was innovative technology in a private house. As Pittsburgh had six mail deliveries a day in 1895, most people still communicated with each other by letter and telegraph.

Bedroom of Adelaide Frick

Full of family photographs, this room is the sanctuary of a devoted wife and mother. When twenty-two-year-old Adelaide Childs married, her mother urged her to "strive to be a good, kind, affectionate and loving wife, giving up your own will for that of your dear husband's." Her

Sentimental, devoted to her husband and children, Adelaide Childs Frick filled her bedroom with family photographs. Her carved walnut bed is no doubt the one in which she gave birth to her four children.

The bathroom adjoining Mrs. Frick's room features plumbing that was considered advanced technology in its time. To care for her clothing and to help her dress in the elaborate fashions of the late nineteenth century, she employed a lady's maid, Pauline Turot.

enameled silver dresser set, gifts from her children, are all engraved with the word "Mamma."

Mrs. Frick's heavily carved walnut furniture dates from shortly after her marriage in 1881. She probably gave birth to her four children in this bed, between 1883 and 1892, for in the nineteenth century only "fallen women" had their babies in hospitals. Her crimson brocade draperies, originally woven to order in 1892 in Lyons, France—"the silk capital of the world"—were rewoven at the Prelle mill there in 1990 from an original pattern in the Prelle archives.

The clothing you see hanging in her closet is typical of her conservative, correct taste. Mrs. Frick, who patronized both Parisian couturiers and Pittsburgh dressmakers, employed a lady's maid to care for her clothes and help her dress for such outings as dinner parties, hospital committee meetings, and picnics with the children. Her clothing shows the same concern for quality and restraint that characterizes Clayton.

Bedroom of Helen Clay Frick

Helen Clay Frick was almost three and a half years old when she began to occupy this sunny room, its walls and ceilings hand-painted with lilacs,

"What I like best is that my bedroom is quite near my dear Mamma's," wrote Helen Clay Frick at age ten. The dolls she and her sister Martha played with were made in France by Jumeau.

roses, chrysanthemums, morning glories, birds, and butterflies. At age ten she wrote that "if all the children had such a pretty room as mine, there would not be any of them sad or unhappy." She added that "what I like best is that my bedroom is quite near my dear Mamma's, and I love to be always near her."

Helen and her father were very close. As she grew up they took long walks together, discussing art and business. In fact, he boasted to his friends about her keen business sense. They often called on the artist Joseph Woodwell, who lived a few blocks away on Penn Avenue. "We . . . spent hours there looking over his most recent pictures and listening to the tales he told of his early years as a student in Paris," she wrote in a memoir about life at Clayton.

Blue Room

For several years Clayton's guest room was occupied by Mrs. Frick's sister and best friend, Martha Childs. The children's beloved "Aunt Attie," she told them stories by the hour. "Neither of us could ever do wrong in her opinion," Helen remembered.

The Blue Room is also where President Theodore Roosevelt rested after his eight-course luncheon at Clayton on July 4, 1902.

Library and Sitting Room

Today we might call this warm, inviting suite "the family room." Only family and a few special friends gathered in this retreat, where the Fricks read, wrote letters, played checkers and backgammon—and dominoes monogrammed "HCF." A child's leather armchair matches the parents'. The library was "where my parents spent the evening when alone, their big arm chairs drawn up in front of the gas-log fire," Helen Frick would remember. "My father often got the 'fidgets' sometime during the evening, and then he and I would take a walk, arm in arm, first on one floor, then on another, steering our way around the furniture and having fun doing it. This seemed to relieve him and then he went early to bed."

The Fricks played whist here with close friends. Andrew Mellon, who would establish the National Gallery in Washington, D.C., after serving as Secretary of the Treasury in the 1920s, often visited on Sundays for conversations about art. Mrs. Frick's social calendar, displayed on her desk,

In their upstairs library and sitting room, the Frick family read, played board games, entertained such close friends as Andrew W. Mellon, and wrote personal letters. The art in these rooms is eclectic and shows Mr. Frick's early preference for peaceful landscapes, portraits, paintings of the Barbizon School—as well as the unusual work of Dagnan-Bouveret. The architect Philip Johnson described these connecting rooms as "one of the best and most interesting nineteenth-century spaces I have been in."

records her engagements for luncheons, dinners, teas, and weddings. Mr. Frick's well-organized desk held ledgers and papers as well as family portraits. A small safe was tucked beneath it.

The decorations in these rooms date from Clayton's 1892 remodeling. Architect Frederick Osterling coordinated the golden oak woodwork with stenciled and painted wall fabric and plush portieres. No doubt following the Fricks' insistence on frugality, he reused the Turkish-style divans they had purchased in the 1880s. For Clayton's restoration the soot-saturated wallcovering was removed, shipped to Paris for cleaning and repair, and returned to Clayton where it was mounted on aluminum panels and rehung.

The variety of the paintings in these rooms is notable. Over the fireplace mantel hangs P.-A.-J. Dagnan-Bouveret's *Christ and the Disciples at Emmaus*, a replica by the artist of a much larger version the Fricks presented to The Carnegie Museum of Art in 1898, in memory of their daughter, Martha.

The fine *Still Life* by William Michael Harnett (1848–1892) depicts homey objects—worn books, sheet music, a Dutch jar, shredded tobacco, meerschaum pipe, and a flute, attributes of a calm, civilized way of life. Mr. Frick bought the painting in 1895. In this photograph it is flanked on the left by a late-nineteenth-century colored-glass vase, cased and cameo-engraved, and on the right by a covered vase of enameled and gilded porcelain, made by the Worcester Royal Porcelain Company in the late nineteenth century in a style evoking the grandeur and sumptuousness of the Italian Renaissance. A Monet landscape, purchased in 1901, also hangs in the library.

Harnett's small *Still Life*, painted in 1890, has hung at Clayton since 1895.

Enclosed Front Porch

The tour ends on the first floor, in this sunny setting enclosed in 1899 to accommodate the orchestrion. Here one can easily imagine the golden afternoons of Helen Clay Frick's childhood . . . and share her nostalgic affection for "the dear old home."

Clayton's front porch was glazed and enclosed in 1899, when the orchestrion was moved here from the parlor. The rattan furniture dates from the same year. The Fricks placed their Christmas tree on the enclosed porch and used the sunny space year-round for informal teas and visiting.

GREENHOUSE AND GROUNDS

BETWEEN August of 1882 and June of 1883, Mr. and Mrs. Frick paid architect Andrew Peebles $50,000 for renovations to their newly acquired house. These improvements included the construction of a greenhouse—for the Fricks wanted their house to be filled with fresh flowers year-round.

The Fricks' greenhouse was used to grow flowers for the house and seedlings for Clayton's flower beds and vegetable gardens, as well as to force bulbs for winter flowering. Over the years the Fricks employed at least two full-time gardeners.

To the Victorians, the love of flowers went hand in hand with "the love of the beautiful" in art and interior design. To appreciate plants was to show a refined aesthetic and moral sensibility for "the children of nature." And, in a time when botanists were discovering new species in the Far East and the tropics, plant collecting demonstrated an appreciation for up-to-date scientific progress. Palms, ferns, and orchids suggested adventures to faraway Africa or the Amazon. Many wealthy families grew tropical plants in conservatories attached to their houses.

The greenhouse you visit today was rebuilt based on one the Fricks constructed in 1897 to replace their 1883 greenhouse. Its 1897 designers were Alden and Harlow of Pittsburgh and Boston, the architects of Andrew Carnegie's new library and museum complex in Oakland. As with the 1893 Phipps Conservatory, the interior fittings were by Lord and Burnham of Irvington-on-Hudson, New York. Mr. and Mrs. Frick regularly opened their greenhouse to the Pittsburgh public, whose love of nature was stimulated by the two conservatories funded by Henry Phipps, an associate of Mr. Frick at Carnegie Steel, as well as by the opening of Schenley Park in 1889.

The Fricks employed a full-time gardener and assistant gardener, who managed both the greenhouse and the grounds. In the greenhouse the

The family opened the greenhouse to the public for spring and fall flower shows of lilies and chrysanthemums. Mr. Frick also indulged his hobby of growing edible mushrooms in the greenhouse basement.

gardeners grew such plants as orchids, chrysanthemums, cyclamens, lilies, and roses. They grew annuals from seed for outdoor bedding and forced bulbs in mid-winter, filling Clayton with the perfume of hyacinths and narcissus on the most dismal January day. In the basement of the greenhouse, Mr. Frick grew edible mushrooms.

Head gardener David Fraser kept the grounds at Clayton from 1896 to 1935. All through the spring, thousands of flowering bulbs created drifts of color—snowdrops, hyacinths, tulips, narcissus, and lily of the valley. In summer, multicolored annuals and perennials such as delphinium, columbines, snapdragons, petunias, ageratum, and nasturtiums grew in beds. There was also a large vegetable garden with beans, beets, cabbage, carrots, cauliflower, many varieties of celery, corn, cucumbers, eggplant, endive, kale, leeks, lettuces, melons, okra, pumpkins, onions, and tomatoes.

Mr. and Mrs. Frick had by the 1890s added five hundred acres to their original acre and a half. They owned fields that stretched to "Holmhurst," the estate owned by their good friends Mr. and Mrs. John Grier Holmes, and bounded by today's Richland Lane and Braddock Avenue. "My father . . . staked out a small private golf course on the hilly portion of his property and sometimes, he and my mother and the Holmes played together," Helen Clay Frick remembered.

Henry Clay Frick and Helen Clay Frick gave most of this land, "Clayton Heights," to Pittsburgh; it is now Frick Park.

Mr. Frick had this building constructed as a playhouse for his children. It was outfitted with children's furniture, and there was a bowling alley behind.

THE CARRIAGE MUSEUM

“IT SEEMS a pity that never again will we see the beautiful ‘turn-outs’ that we had in the old days,’’ Helen Clay Frick would write nostalgically in 1954, remembering the majestic, high-stepping horses who pulled the Frick family’s various stylish carriages. Just as Victorian etiquette demanded a specialized fork for every course at dinner, and the proper clothes for every hour of the day and night, so it was important to drive the right vehicle at the right time. Mr. and Mrs. Frick owned a proper assortment of conveyances.

The brougham, for example, “was the handsome closed carriage in which my mother usually drove about,’’ Miss Frick explained. “It held three people, but there were other carriages that held more, and of these, the ‘wagonette’ was my favorite. In it, we sometimes took our picnic suppers to a specially lovely spot in Swissvale, so named because it bore resemblance to Switzerland.’’ Mr. and Mrs. Frick bought the brougham in New York on their wedding trip, in December 1881, along with “1 set heavy Single Harness with whole bkles, small loops & brass furniture all over’’ for $225. That year, too, Mr. Frick paid $900 for a team of black horses—expensive by the standards of the day.

The Fricks kept two pairs of horses, all over sixteen hands, or sixty-four inches, high. Recalled Miss Frick, “For a long time there were two bays, ‘General’ and ‘Major,’ and two chestnuts, ‘King George’ and ‘King James.’ They were great pets and very stunning besides. . . . There was also a very fast trotter, ‘Fred M,’ the gift of Mr. [Philander] Knox to my mother. How she enjoyed driving him on the boulevard and letting him travel at full speed.

C. BECKERT, Jr.
HAY, GRAIN, FEED, &c.
No. 1520 Fifth Ave.
Pittsburg, Pa.

Helen Clay Frick, driving her Welsh ponies, "Countess" and "Violet." With her are her governess, Mlle. Marika Ogiz, and the family's coachman, James Elmore.

"Not the least important were my two ponies, 'Countess' and 'Violet,' presented to me by [U.S.] Senator [J. Donald] Cameron. They were beautiful Welsh ponies, full sisters thirteen hands high, and for many years they were my greatest joy. I had a specially built trap holding two with a rumble behind for the coachman, and several times a week I drove them through the parks and along the boulevards." Miss Frick's trap was called a spider phaeton. The word "phaeton" comes from the Greek myth about Phaëthon—the son of Helios, god of the sun—who all too proudly attempted to drive his father's chariot.

The Fricks, who enjoyed music, used their six-passenger "opera bus" to go to concerts by the Pittsburgh Symphony Orchestra, conducted from 1898 to 1904 by Victor Herbert, at Carnegie Music Hall. They also attended performances by visiting opera companies—the Metropolitan Opera regularly toured to Pittsburgh, with such top artists as Enrico Caruso and Emma Calvé.

In all, the Fricks probably kept between five and ten horses at their Clayton stable. Until the arrival of James Elmore from Philadelphia in 1895, they employed various coachmen. Elmore was a highly trained coachman who took over the complete management of the stables. Helen adored him, for he would drive around her dolls with the same serious propriety with which he drove all the Fricks.

With his lifelong interest in new technology, Mr. Frick took to the automobile before the turn of the century. "My father was the first owner of a foreign 'machine,' as they were then called," Miss Frick wrote. "It was a Mercedes, purchased in Paris in the fall of 1898, and he brought over a French chauffeur, Georges Désprès, at the same time to drive it. The chassis of the car was bright red and it was known throughout Pittsburgh as the 'red devil.' Georges was a beautiful driver but he loved to speed and so did my father. It took them only fifteen minutes to reach the office downtown. However, there were many drawbacks to motoring in those early days, for there were very few automobiles and the horses were so frightened of them that it was often necessary for Georges to stop the car, get out, and lead the horses past the puffing monster."

THE FRICK ART MUSEUM

HELEN CLAY FRICK built this intimate, personal museum in 1970 as a gift to Pittsburgh. Both she and her father, who established The Frick Collection in New York, believed that works of art are best displayed in surroundings that evoke a well-appointed home. Fresh flowers from the greenhouse welcome visitors and enhance the charm of The Frick Art Museum—now the site for changing exhibitions of paintings, drawings, sculpture, and decorative arts. At The Frick Art Museum you enjoy relaxed encounters with the great art of the past.

The Italian Renaissance-style museum is built of Alabama limestone, marble from Italy and Portugal, Mexican tile, Burmese and African teak, American walnut, and Honduras mahogany. Growing up at the turn of the century, Miss Frick would certainly have been attracted to Renaissance architecture—for tastemakers then considered the Italian Renaissance the greatest period in art history.

Miss Frick's own art makes up the museum's permanent collection, displayed on velvet and damask wallcoverings. Among the treasures to be enjoyed here is a collection of Sienese and Florentine fourteenth- and fifteenth-century paintings, featuring rare works by Duccio, Sassetta, and Giovanni di Paolo. Other notable paintings include a devotional diptych by Jean Bellegambe, Antoine Le Nain's *Le Bénédicité*, a pastorale by François Boucher, Jan Steen's *The Music Lesson*, and works by Hubert Robert. One of the most enchanting works is a terra cotta bust of his wife by Jean-Antoine Houdon. Interestingly, many of the paintings depict loving scenes of family life as well as nature—ideals for Miss Frick throughout her life.

Holding center stage in the oval rotunda, with its curved, luminous

François Boucher,
French, 1703–1770
Pastorale: A Peasant Boy Fishing
Oil on canvas
95 x 67 in. (241.2 x 170.2 cm.)

Teakwood columns in the rotunda frame a fifty-three-inch-tall rococo marble urn sculpted in 1782 by Claude Michel, known as Clodion (1738–1814).

ceiling, is a carved marble eighteenth-century urn by the French sculptor Claude Michel, called Clodion. It is one of a set made for the terrace of the palace of Versailles, two of which are in the National Gallery of Art. On the walls hang French and Flemish tapestries, including two large fragments in the millefleurs tradition, woven in the Loire Valley about 1500. One depicts a rare musical concert theme.

The Gallery of Italian Art features paintings by Arcangelo di Cola da Camerino (1385–1450), Duccio di Buoninsegna (ca. 1278–1319), Giovanni di Paolo (1403–1483), and Stefano di Giovanni, called Sassetta (1391/1400–1450).

Sassetta, who painted in Siena in the fifteenth century, was a contemporary of Fra Angelico. His *Madonna and Child with Two Angels* (ca. 1424) inspired art historian Walter Read Hovey to write, "Rarely has the style of a work so beautifully reflected the pure, uncluttered spirit of a religious ideal." His Madonna "is the Queen of Heaven but possesses the humble sentiment of a human mother."

The *Nativity* of Giovanni di Paolo brings the charm of court and aristocratic patronage into religious art. The style is similar to the ordinary scenes of daily life found in illuminated manuscripts such as the *Trés Riches Heures* of the Duc de Berry.

On green velvet walls in the gallery to the right of the rotunda hang paintings from the early sixteenth to the nineteenth centuries. Notable is

Opposite page, top:
Images of art and nature—themes that echo throughout The Frick Art & Historical Center—enhance the appeal of this unusual millefleurs tapestry, one of two large fragments in The Frick Art Museum's permanent collection.

Opposite page, bottom:
In the Gallery of Italian Art, visitors enjoy paintings from the fourteenth and fifteenth centuries. Like most works in the museum, they are from Helen Clay Frick's personal art collection.

Annunciation, by the fifteenth-century Sienese painter Stefano di Giovanni, called Sassetta, is in tempera on panels (4½ x 6 in.), which formed the pinnacles of a small altarpiece.

Le Bénédicité by the French artist Antoine Le Nain (1588–1648). Painted in oil on copper, this tiny genre scene of a family at prayer is a remarkable example of Northern realism.

The Frick Art Museum also features three paintings by Hubert Robert (1733–1808). The first keeper of the Louvre after the French Revolution, he worked at a time when people were just becoming interested in the classical Greco-Roman past and the emerging romanticism, and saw beauty in fallen classical columns and architraves. An example is his *Adoration of the Magi*, in which the manger as a classical building in ruin suggests the old order giving way to the new. Especially important are his paintings of the gardens at Versailles, for he was commissioned to design a romantic grotto there in 1778. Two of The Frick Art Museum's Robert paintings, *Le Bosquet des Bains d'Apollon, Versailles* and *Le Jardin Elysée du Musée des Monuments Français*, formerly hung in the Pavlovsk Palace near St. Petersburg.

Giovanni di Paolo painted this Nativity scene ca. 1436–1440. It depicts the concept of the Christian Trinity, the Adoration of the Virgin, the Adoration of the Shepherds, the shepherds' journey to Bethlehem, and that of the Wise Men.

Hubert Robert, 1733–1808
Le Bosquet des Bains d'Apollon, Versailles
Oil on canvas
24 7/8 x 31 3/8 in. (63.2 x 79.7 cm.)

Antoine Le Nain, 1588–1648
Le Bénédicité
Oil on copper
5⅝ x 7 in. (14.3 x 17.8 cm.)

Beyond the galleries of the permanent collection are those for traveling art exhibitions of international renown.

Always a New Experience

The Frick Art Museum is an ever-renewing source of pleasure. The museum presents a continuous program of traveling exhibitions of art from museums and private collections around the world—often never before seen in the United States. These distinctive shows offer visitors the opportunity to enjoy great paintings, Old Master drawings, and priceless objects in a serene, contemplative setting.

Exhibitions the museum has presented include The Harold Samuel Collection: Seventeenth-Century Dutch and Flemish Paintings from Mansion House, London; The Art of the Himalayas: Treasures from Nepal and Tibet; The Real and the Spiritual: Nineteenth-Century French Drawings from the Musée des Beaux-Arts de Lyon; Old Master Drawings from Chatsworth; Inigo Jones: Complete Architectural Drawings; Russian Icons of the Golden Age, 1400–1700; and many more.

Great art enjoyed in personal, inviting surroundings . . . this is just part of a visit to Helen Clay Frick's legacy to Pittsburgh. She hoped that countless visitors would gain some share of her abiding appreciation for the civilized values of an earlier time.

In sharing both her home and her personal art collection with visitors she would never know, Helen Clay Frick followed in the footsteps of her father. Hers is an enduring gift that enhances the arts of an entire region and the lives of thousands.

Author's Acknowledgments

Careful historical research, scholarship, and documentation preceded the writing of this text, including work by Kahren Jones Arbitman, Lu Donnelly, Walter Read Hovey, Joanne B. Moore, Ellen M. Rosenthal, Louise F. Wells, and others. I am especially grateful to Dennis Ciccone for asking me to be part of this project, and to DeCourcy E. McIntosh, John Thomas, Lisa Hubeny, and Nadine Grabania for their knowledge and help.